THE ART OF BEING A
SCHOOL
COUNSELOR

Leading with Confidence, Compassion, and Authenticity

NANCY L. REGAS
M.S., M.F.T., P.P.S.

outskirts
press

Table of Contents

Acknowledgements

To all of you who called me your counselor, this book is my heart-felt thank you to each of you. Please know it was my privilege to share your individual journey, and to have you put your trust in me while you were on the pathway towards a high school diploma. Sharing your laughter, tears, joy, sorrow, setbacks, and accomplishments are etched into my soul forever.

To my granddaughters, I only hope you have a counselor you can go to for anything and that you feel safe and heard in a trusting relationship. Also, a counselor who guides you throughout the process so you can transform your dreams into reality. Through that relationship, may you also learn the power of honesty, integrity, respect, and caring.

To my husband, the most masterful teacher and administrator, thank you for lighting the education road for me so brilliantly and for your unconditional support, encouragement, and belief in me.

To my daughters, it was pure joy to watch and guide you through your amazing journeys. You kept me awestruck while I observed and admired your experience.

Finally, to the many associates throughout my journey in education who went from colleagues to be my dear friends.

To all of you, THANK YOU from the bottom of my heart.

Foreword by Dr. Rebecca Fink

AS A NERVOUS freshman with her arm in a sling from recent shoulder surgery, I stepped onto the campus of Patrick Henry High School in San Diego for the first day of classes to begin the requisite journey that would culminate in graduation and university placement. By virtue of my last name, I had briefly met my assigned guidance counselor, Mrs. Nancy Regas.

With chance encounters, it is hard to predict the impact individuals will have on you, from teaching valuable lessons to making you stronger to encouraging you to achieve beyond your self-imposed limits. Whether brief or long-term, motivating or challenging, each interaction has a role and purpose in your life. Such is the case with school guidance counselors, who shepherd students for a quadrennium, serving as navigator, cheerleader, advisor, disciplinarian, and advocate. Mrs. Regas excelled in her role, and her mentorship, friendship, and support carried forward well beyond high school as she followed my journey through academics and into the working world as a pediatrician.

The Regas culture of compassion and selflessness extends to her personal family as well. As a medical student living on the East Coast and away from my family, Mrs. Regas did not hesitate to put me in touch with her daughter and family who lived nearby and who "adopted" me and ensured I always had a place to land, especially during the holidays. Over the next few years, as I moved to the Midwest for residency and finally back to the West Coast for employment, I continued to value our conversations, which were always, and continue to be, filled with love, encouragement, and support.

Mrs. Regas has had a profound influence on my life, for which I will be forever grateful. It is my hope that you will consider and value her perspective and wisdom in artfully crafting approaches that will speak to the strengths and challenges of each unique student who will look to you for guidance. And at the end of each day, in the Regas way, don't forget to live, laugh, and love.

Chapter 1

My Evolution Towards Becoming A School Counselor

I **LOVED HIGH** school. I loved learning, my teachers, being involved, and being a leader. After college, I got married to a teacher, and I watched his pure joy working with students; he seemed to be energized by creating a unique world within his classroom. Despite that love of school, when I went to graduate school, I chose not to track towards a P.P.S. [Pupil Personnel Services Credential] preparing me to work in schools but took the M.F.T. [Marriage and Family Therapist] track instead. At the time, I believed it was the right path for me. Once I got my license and began working, disappointedly, it wasn't what I had conceived in my mind. So, after four years in private practice, I went back to school to earn my P.P.S., and truly, that is when the light bulb went on for me. In one of my classes, the professor said a sentence that would change the trajectory of my life and put everything thus far into perspective: "a career is an expression of who you are." That was it; every path I had previously taken now seemed like steppingstones to my future. In another class, we were divided into teams, each group becoming a school; the task at hand was to present the school's counseling program to the board to secure funding. Being named principal in my group, my responsibility was presenting our vision and mission of the counseling office, its staff, and the budget required to get the job done. Afterward, an actual principal on the panel told me he was very impressed and asked how long I had worked for the district. When I replied, two years, he was stunned. He told me I knew and understood more of what schools needed than some of his colleagues who had been with the district 20+ years. I went home that night beaming. I had found my true calling.

My first job with the district was as the Resource Coordinator of a Violence/Substance Abuse Prevention Project for Pregnant/Parenting Teens [yes, that was my exact title]. I remember the interview with the Director of the Alternative Education Department and the Project Manager for SANDAPP [San Diego Adolescent Pregnancy and Parenting Program]. She asked me a plethora of intense questions; despite internally quivering, I rapidly fired off responses. After an hour and a half, she stopped, smiled, looked at her boss and said, "I want her." I smiled on the outside but on the inside, I was cheering and doing my happy dance! I felt as if I had arrived and was totally validated.

The first day on the job, I was taken into the workroom/copy room/lunchroom/meeting room and now add MY office. There was a desk in the corner with no drawers, just one open cupboard and a telephone. My director said, "Ok, start calling people," and then closed the door behind her. I sat at the desk and thought, what have I gotten myself into? This was a brand-new position in the school district, with no guidelines or predecessor. The State of California's Maternal Child Health Department grant was the only instruction. I thought, who am I supposed to call? No one knows me or will know what I am talking about. So, I started making a list of agencies to call and began to set the wheels in motion. "Hello, I'm Nancy Regas and I'm the Resource Coordinator… [you can finish the rest]." "Who?" I'd repeat and explain. Slowly, I started making headway. Fast forward two and a half years when I gave the final presentation to the regional directors and project managers. [We had received notification the state was ending the grant. The sad reality is "soft money" is often at the whim of those in charge]. When I told my story and described my first day, I ended with "and now people are calling me." The position gave me so much confidence, fueled my passion, nurtured my speaking skills, and gave me a voice I didn't know I had. I will always be grateful to Hazel Welbourne, the amazing woman who gave me a chance.

After being put in a new position that turned out to be abusive and consequently so overwhelming [I will spare you the ugly details], I moved into being a life skills counselor. I had an amazing partner, and we traveled to the elementary, middle, and high schools in the Tierrasanta area of San Diego. My passion for public speaking soared, and I learned how to reach students at each level. Hearing their stories not only inspired and challenged me but lit my pathway. I also learned that even though I focused on students, I had to be conscious of winning over, listening to, and relating to administrators, teachers, and parents. Counselors have the difficult job of making and keeping four entities happy: students, parents, administrators, and teachers and to be prepared for the reality that they are often all not on the same page!

During my time as a life skills counselor, I completed my P.P.S. Credential, and then took a counselor position at one school, no more traveling. Amazingly to my good fortune, I landed five minutes from my home, and high school was where I chose to be. My decision was questioned by several administrators in the district that knew my passions and my journey, as they said, "High school counselors don't counsel, they just schedule classes; are you sure you want to do that?" I replied, "That <u>may</u> be what other counselors do, but that's not the kind of counselor I will be; I <u>will</u> counsel students."

So why am I writing this book? It is because despite retiring, I still hold the same passion and fervor for the one-on-one relationship with adolescents on their journey towards high school graduation and adulthood. Speaking with some counselors, I believe their passion is missing; trust me, it is the *key* to becoming an effective and successful school counselor. I believe in the current society with so many challenges and high demands for performance [and now a pandemic], often personal issues are overlooked; yet underneath, they're expected to be addressed. The increase in depression, anxiety, bullying, single-parent homes, parents working two jobs to make ends meet, remarried families with new sets of challenges regarding step-parenting and stepchildren is daunting in my estimation. The COVID reality of school at home/online has complicated things even more. Students <u>need</u> a caring, compassionate counselor. I hope that if you are struggling with your role or just starting your career, this book will help you transform your job into a haven for young people, as well as, fulfill you as a professional. For *all* other educators, may this illuminate the role of the counselor and deepen collaboration for the benefit of *all* students.

Chapter 2

Establishing Your Identity As A School Counselor

ON MY FIRST day in my office [which was very small], I was working at the computer. The window was open, and my back was to it. Suddenly, I heard, "Mrs. Regas," which startled me because no one was at my door. When I turned and looked up, a student was literally leaning his entire torso in the open window into my office and began asking me a question. I said good morning and told the student to come into my office to have the conversation. Throughout the week, I had other students do the same thing; when I finally asked, "Why don't you students come into my office to talk?" Their response was the same, "Because our last counselor didn't want us to." I was stunned; it took me a month, but I finally established that I didn't do "walk by counseling" as I labeled it, and word traveled fast that

Mrs. Regas had an open-door policy. A counselor's office should be a safe zone for students; they shouldn't be made to feel as if they are a bother or unwanted. If a student comes at an inappropriate time [out of class without a pass, interrupts a present conversation or phone call, or you are under pressure for a deadline], clearly, but kindly let the student know this is not a good time and then let them know <u>when</u> they can return. Never say, come back later because "your later" and "their later" may not coincide. The open-door policy creates a trust factor so important in working with adolescents. I wanted my students to get to know me as much as me getting to know them. When that happens, the dialogue is much richer, more honest, and revealing, as well as gratifying to both parties.

Being ready to see students when they start arriving is another policy, I believe is vital; it is why I *always* got to work one to one and a half hours before the start of the school day for students. The quiet of the early morning is something I always savored [and still do]. My computer was up and running, I answered emails, wrote emails, listened to my phone messages, and set a "flexible" agenda for my day; it was all at my pace before the unknown began to reveal itself. Students knew I was there early and if they were willing to give up their time [i.e., time away from their cell phones, their friends, getting a morning coffee, just hanging out and listening to music, or sleeping longer], I wanted to reward that by welcoming them into my office, their safe space [and their source of Hershey Nuggets]. A student had my full attention when she/he was with me, so we often got a lot accomplished in a shorter amount of time, or at least set the stage for the next visit. I cherished those one-on-one moments. I wanted to be the kind of counselor I didn't have in high school. Honestly, as much as I loved school and being involved with several extracurricular activities, I only remember a handful of times going into the "guidance office," as it was named at my school, only to pick up something. I cannot recall my counselor's name nor remember any deep conversations. Contrast this with me having former students now adults, contact me, meet me for coffee, and joyously greet me when we run into each other. I cherish seeing former students and hearing their life stories; I consider it a privilege indeed.

Another part of your identity is how you speak to students. Especially when working with adolescents, you have to know what you are saying and why, as well as be prepared to give them a reasonable explanation. The more information you provide to them/for them, the better your rapport will be. Adolescents challenge adults when they believe what they are being told is unreasonable, unclear, or in their mind, doesn't make any sense. You have to take your adult frame of reference and transpose it to a teenage frame of reference until they have their aha moment. In doing this, never talk down to them. Instead, talk with them, to them, and about them. Remember what you say can turn someone's life upside down or right side up. It's <u>your</u> office, so you set the tone, pace, and respect level.

Respect is key. You don't have to like someone to respect them. My office walls were covered with sayings, messages, and pictures that I used as teaching tools. I would often point to something and ask my student to read it out loud and then the dialogue began. It was always something that explained, revealed, inspired, challenged, or validated our conversation. Especially if the conversation got emotional, the objectivity of words in print helped the student collect themselves while taking a personal look. A large poster had a series of faces with different expressions [what we would now refer to as emoticons]. When a student struggled with sharing their feelings, I would ask them to look at the poster and select a face that represented them at the moment. Students always complied and quickly found "their face" upon the wall. Then the flood gates could and would open, and other feelings and descriptions emerged. Another message on my board was the word **RESPECT** printed in bold, bright colors and large font. I would tell students that was my favorite word. Particularly in our current society where things have gotten extremely hostile with individuals [especially in cyberspace] believing they can say anything to or about anyone no matter how rude or demeaning it is. The 45th president's constant name calling was of great concern to me. He practiced everything I taught my students not to do, and his actions have left an indelible scar on this country and its citizens. We must be better than that and realize words matter, and they can leave a permanent scar or a positive imprint. When I was growing up the following expression was popular: "Sticks and stones will break my bones, but names will never hurt me." I used to think [and it was confirmed by adult sources] no matter what was said to me, I could protect myself and it didn't have to penetrate my exterior and take up residence in my interior. During my time of counseling students, I saw another side of that. I listened to stories about the reality and results of name-calling. I vividly remember a 15-year-old female with a 2-year-old son; she was in a parenting class I was teaching when I worked for SANDAPP. I can still feel the sting of her words: "My mother calls me a B____ every day of my life, and you are going to tell me how to raise my son?!?!?" I worked very hard to validate her reality while explaining that I was there to support her, not condemn her. It's amazing the things we forget and the things we try to but can't.

Here's another example of how we are imprinted. I was visiting a school and doing a presentation to a class on teen relationship violence. A female raised her hand and asked if I was married. She said, "Your husband calls you names." I replied no. I explained that we disagreed, even argued, but never called each other names. She shrugged her shoulders and then said, "A boyfriend called you names." I replied no again. She responded with exasperation, "I don't know anyone like you; you're just old." I calmly validated her reality while offering another way, which is why I was there to speak. The bell rang, and she turned and never looked back. I will never know if my words impacted her to seek relationships of equality and respect. This is where I knew I was a seed planter, not always knowing if what was planted would take root, sprout, flourish, or wither and die. It committed me to be very deliberate with my word choice; I also became very purposeful in teaching students how to control all the words left on *their* personal doorstep, instead of letting those words navigate their life's journey and beliefs. The world wide web complicates this.

The internet is a blessing and a curse. Who doesn't like instant information? I was stunned when I asked a question, and my then 5-year-old granddaughter told me to "just google it." Her world is so different from mine at her age. It is imperative we all remember that cyberspace is <u>public and permanent, not private and temporary</u>. The veil of anonymity can quickly be removed revealing the source. The news is filled with information being exposed from a person's past, only to come back and haunt them when they run for political office. The lessons of cyberspace, i.e., respect and integrity, must be taught <u>continuously;</u> and as a counselor, you are one of the primary teachers, guides, and role models.

Each level of school counseling, i.e., elementary,

middle, and high school, has to be conducted within the developmental stature of its students: you don't want to talk down to a high schooler or be so above the clouds for an elementary student that they have no clue what you are saying. Balance and understanding are key. When working with adolescents, a counselor should be cordial and approachable; however, that is not the same as being their friend. You are *not* their peer or buddy. At first, that may sound harsh, nevertheless or regardless [two of my favorite words which we will come back to shortly], it *is* the truth. Being perceived as their friend will compromise your ability to say no, set boundaries, deliver consequences, or establish guidelines. If a counselor crosses the line into friendship, the student will likely challenge their words or directions, and may even take them less seriously. If a counselor delivers any form of guidance with friendliness and care, it will be received, as it was given, with authenticity.

Now let's get back to two words all counselors should have in their arsenal: nevertheless and regardless. There is a huge difference between those words and the often relied upon "but." The word but just about erases everything that comes before it. So, an individual says, "I love you, but you hurt my feelings." The I love you gets lost and dismissed; the focus becomes the hurt, the pain caused, and who is to blame. On the other hand, if the same person says I love you, nevertheless, my feelings were hurt by your actions.

The love is still there. She/he can still accept the love, which will actually be their safeguard when they confront the hurt. Nevertheless or regardless unabashedly says the first part of the sentence is true, real, and needs to be validated. The use of one of those words will keep your recipient listening and trusting you, which is crucial for any counselor. The use of the word but changes the entire message, the delivery, and the receipt. Try it and you will see!

Before we move on, close the book and study the picture on the front cover. It is a painting my youngest daughter lovingly gifted us with one Christmas. She knew how much I loved the work of the artist Jackson Pollock. Her painting has brought us much joy and pride in her talent. I always excitedly declare to guests, "It's *not* a Pollock, it's *a* <u>Regas</u>!" I love to stare at it and try to follow a line. School Counseling is a lot like that painting; it is not a straight line from point a to point z. You don't start the day with a full inbox and end the day with an empty one. Each encounter will take you on a different journey; you have to be prepared to keep moving in order to give your student what they need at the moment, as well as, what they deserve: specialized and focused attention that sees them for who they are right then, right there. Everything is taken into consideration, which ultimately conveys to the student they truly have been heard and validated. Please don't misunderstand what I am saying; this does not mean you condone poor behavior or tolerate lying or cheating. However, it does mean you are open and honest to receive them; you are moving them to become the best of themselves while simultaneously giving the best of yourself. You must follow their lead to accurately comprehend the situation before you while establishing healthy boundaries for them and yourself. Yes, you have to learn how to juggle and become a *school counseling artist*.

No two days are the same; it's almost analogous to getting and opening a present each day where you honestly have no clue what's inside!

With all of that, now you know why you go home at the end of the day exhilarated <u>and</u> exhausted!

Chapter 3

Do You Know What School Is Really About?

WHEN I WORKED, I endeavored to find ways to relate to students, demystify the counselor/student relationship while empowering them to take charge of their school career. High school is a microcosm of the adult world. If students and parents are locked into the description that school is about Math, Science, English, and History, students will lose the ability to transfer skills, and parents will grow in frustration. It becomes really difficult when a student doesn't particularly like or struggles with a specific class/subject. Here are the seven characteristics that I believe constitute what school is *really* about: time management, organization, responsibility, accountability, accessing resources, knowing when and whom to ask for help, and punctuality. School uses Math, Science, English, and History [and of course the Arts] to teach those seven things. If a student learns those powerful lessons, they will make it anywhere, as those are "transferable skills" to college, to the job market, to life. If they do not learn those seven skills, they will struggle and falter no matter how vast their brilliance. Counselors need to help students identify those characteristics in themselves, their strengths, and their shortfalls; this way, they will know what to work on and how. Let's explore them one by one.

Time management starts to become a factor in middle school. Suddenly a student has six teachers who don't ask the question, "Did another teacher give you an assignment for tonight? If yes, I will postpone mine." [Yah, right?!?!] Every class is an island onto itself, a self-contained unit that has expectations. Students have to learn to use their time to get through all six of those courses simultaneously and successfully.

Organization is the ability to prioritize things. Let's say there's a test tomorrow in a difficult subject; plus, in a book being discussed in a favorite class, you are assigned to read three chapters and answer questions by the end of the week. Students often do the thing they like the most first and save the least favorite or most difficult for last. The problem with that is twofold: one, they may run out of time, and two, by the time they get to the last item, it may be during their lowest energy point. Students have to learn when they have the most energy and then prioritize their tasks so that the most difficult is accomplished during that time frame. Some students need a break after school, while others need to keep the ball rolling while they have momentum. Other students are often recharged after dinner. Knowing these aspects about oneself, in conjunction with using a planner/agenda, organization becomes a great asset.

The second part of organization is remembering what to take to school every single day. I was always stunned when I enrolled a new student who was planning on starting school that day and seeing they brought nothing with them: no pencil, pen, paper, binder, etc. I would ask how they expected to do their job without any tools. Sometimes when a student was so disorganized, I would have them empty their backpack in my office [at times, not a pretty sight] and we would go piece by piece. Sadly, one student had a twinkie, a coloring book, and a pencil. My heart broke as I realized this was going to be a very long process; hence, I always kept some supplies available to give to students to get them started. So, all of that said, I started using the acronym P.A.N.T.S. I would start by asking the question, "Would you come to school without your pants?" I'd get a gasp, a chuckle, a DUH, an emphatic no, or some combination of all of the above. Then I would ask, "Then why do you come to school without them?" and explain the following.

P = Parent notes/messages; A= Assignments; N = Notebook; T = Textbooks; S= Supplies. Every night a student needs to check their backpack and make sure it is filled with their P.A.N.T.S.; then, in the morning which can often be hectic [especially for slow starters, students being dropped off by working parents possibly including siblings at different schools/ times, or being picked up or picking up others for a carpool], all they have to grab is one thing, i.e., their backpack. It makes getting to school much calmer, and yes, organized throughout the entire day. Speaking of backpacks, help your students realize they should never throw anything away until the end of the year. This prepares the student for several possibilities: a grade accidentally was not recorded, one assignment becoming the foundation or catalyst for another project, or a final exam being cumulative where many assignments become useful study guides. Keeping a place at home where the student maintains individual folders for each class is also a vital component of organization. Every week, every couple of weeks, or at the end of a particular topic of study, the student can clean out their notebook [which is probably bulging at the seams] and their backpack; this will keep it much lighter to carry around, as well as, assist the student in finding current information, notes, and assignments.

Responsibility is incremental in that the older you are, the more responsibility is thrust upon you. I used to tell parents and students that in elementary school they held your hand; in middle school, they let go of your hand but stood right next to you guiding you along. In high school, they are waiting at their door for you to enter; in college, they are in a building, and your job is to find the right one to enter. All of that says with each developmental milestone, you can do more and have more independence, yet built into that are more obligations.

Accountability is sometimes a difficult concept to help adolescents latch onto. With their newfound "freedoms" enhancing their independence, they often function with the following mindset: I am self-sufficient; therefore, I don't need assistance, and I don't need to keep you in the loop! Learning that self-sufficiency doesn't equate to isolation is a challenge. Adolescents desperately want to prove to their parents, their teachers, or any other authority figure, they can handle whatever is before them. That may be very true, however, when answerability is on the table, it creates alertness in the student as well as keeps them on their toes. Knowing they have to explain their decisions, their accomplishments, and their progress is a way to keep them focused and directed. Remember, the stakes are higher now and will continue to increase in college and the workplace.

Accessing resources is such an important factor in critical thinking. When I was growing up, I remember when my father purchased a set of the Encyclopedia

Britannica. My brother and I felt as if we had the world in our home. Now, of course, the world is truly at one's fingertips with the world wide web. The amount of information is at times overwhelming. School is about so much more than facts. To meet one's goals, the individual has to determine what information to use, how to use it, and then, where to find it. To obtain that information, if the wrong resource is chosen or used in the wrong way, goals will be delayed or detoured. The student also has to know what resources are available in each classroom, school-wide, and what they have at home. Resources, however, are only valuable *if* they are utilized.

Knowing when and whom to ask for help breaks the mindset described earlier that self-sufficiency or independence means not needing anyone else. The reality of life is that every human being needs help at various times in their lives which is the key point in this paragraph. When is the time to reach out and to whom? As a counselor, you are the one to assist a student in deciphering how to figure this out. A counselor is the hub of the wheel connecting the student to all of the spokes surrounding the wheel. Problem-solving is the tool that enhances this process. First and foremost, it is important to stress one cannot skip a step during problem-solving.

Step one, the problem has to be defined without which one may be solving the wrong issue. Step two, uncensored brainstorming of all the possible options occurs: that means no comments like, "that's stupid, that will take too long, done that before, or it's too hard," to name a few. Censoring establishes roadblocks before you've even begun. Step three is selecting the best possible choice for that time and that circumstance, allowing a student to claim they did the best they knew how at the time. Step four is the implementation of the selected option. One has to dive in to see if it works. Finally, after implementation, evaluation *has* to occur: Is the problem solved? Did it work effectively? Can I move on? If the answers are yes, then bravo. If any one of the answers is no, then it's back to step three, selecting another option. Unraveling this problem-solving methodology with a student is intensive, challenging, and may require a great deal of patience; however, when the light bulb goes on, as they say, it is so rewarding for both the student and the counselor.

Finally, we have punctuality. I used to have a sign in my office that read: "Early is on time, you are ready to start. On time is late, you have missed something. Late is totally unacceptable." This may take a long time to teach but it is so important. Being able to get to class, sit down, take out a book, an assignment, and a planner, *before* the bell rings creates an internal message where the student says, I'm all in, I'm ready for anything; there is an inner calm. On the other hand, walking into class *as* the bell rings, a student starts class scrambling frantically. They are rushing to find their seat, get out materials, turn something in, and they aren't focused on the words the teacher is speaking. The result is always being a step behind. Finally, being late is disruptive to the teacher, the class, and to one's sense of self; it just seems as if the student never fully connects with the totality of the class experience.

The entire impact of these seven attributes is so powerful and carries any student the rest of their lives: in college, in relationships, and in the workplace. That is why they are so vital to an individual's success and well-being; it is also why they <u>must</u> be the ultimate goals of the school experience [the ends of learning] to be developed through the subjects taught in each and every class [the means to learning].

Chapter 4

The Personal Side Of The Counselor/ Student Relationship

AS A COUNSELOR, you have the opportunity to foster the development of a student's experience. Expectations are vital but not in the way you might think. It's not that you expect a student to be perfect, get all A's, be the best, but you expect them to be *the best version of themselves*. You expect honesty and respect, accept nothing less, and give nothing less to them. I always told students there were two things I detested and that was being lied to and being lied about. A distrust is immediately created, and it is so difficult to move beyond apprehension. One day a teacher called me and stated she was confirming our student had been in my office the previous day. I informed her that wasn't possible since I was out of the office at a seminar [he had skipped class and claimed he was with me]. I told her to send him to me after class. When he entered my office, I asked him what he thought about the workshop he attended the previous day. He quickly refuted attending any workshop. I said I found that surprising since he told his teacher he was with me and I was at an all-day seminar. His head immediately hung low. Busted! I stated that I would not support him or help him if he was lying as I won't back up a lie. Then we began the conversation anew, moving beyond this and repairing the situation with his teacher and me, which included apologies. You see, honesty and respect are the foundational blocks of any trusting relationship. The student knows if they fall, you will be there to support them getting back up and moving forward. Everyone needs to know there is someone in their corner cheering them on through the highs and lows of their journey. It is such a privilege to be that person. I often looked back on moments in my own life when I thought a counselor would have been so beneficial. Never underestimate the impact your words, your presence, your attention, your listening, and your smile has on an adolescent. They want so much to be seen and heard for who they are. As a result, I tried to develop key words or phrases that would say a lot with a few words in order to capture their attention. One of those words was "Nike."

When I would sit with a student and they would

"yes, but" every suggestion I had, I often interjected an emphatic Nike. If they had been through this with me before, sometimes I would get the eye rolls and hear "Just do it" with a groan. It was like a giant road-block to their naysaying was removed, and the "but" also disappeared; then, I could reframe the dialogue. I took them back to brainstorming, helped them re-state options [or even create new ones], and finally had them purposefully choose the best one for them. I often marveled at the power of that simple four-letter word. It took a cultural reference and transformed it into a catalyst for action.

Another tool exposes the truth about an error and what comes next, i.e., which direction of the fork in the road they will go: the way of the mistake or the way of the experience. It IS a choice and *totally under their control*. A mistake is repeating the same error over and over, so nothing is learned, nothing is gained. It is often claimed the definition of insanity is doing the same thing and expecting different results. Experience is the steppingstone saying, "been there, done that, not going to do it again." Sometimes it means once again going back to the brainstorming portion of problem-solving and finding another option. The reality is that experience is growth-producing, a move forward, no matter how large or small. Since adolescents often feel they have no choice, as counselors, we must always remind them while change is inevitable and happens outside of their control, growth is an option they can

<u>always</u> choose.

Friendship is quite a big deal during adolescence; at times, social media diminishes the depth of true friendships with the superficiality of "likes." What is a like anyway? What does it really mean? When I taught about teen relationship violence, I would discuss the word intimacy. The best definition I ever heard was "in to see me." A real friend accepts all of you. Before counting how many likes you have, it is important to assist adolescents in becoming their own best friend and not their own worst enemy. They have to learn to ask themselves questions. One of the ways is S.T.A.R. [Stop, Think, Act, Review] that I learned in a behavior modification workshop. As a physical reminder, I designed a business-size card with a star and the acronym. It reinforced the concept and empowered them to recognize they did own a "personal" remote control. We want to learn how to become a person of action as opposed to reaction. With that said, of course I am fully aware there are circumstances in life where we need quick reactions: swerving away from a car out of control, stepping back onto a curb when a car approaches and doesn't see you, the pedestrian, or pulling your hands away from anything hot, to name a few. Nevertheless, it is crucial to know we have options. To use S.T.A.R., there is an event that occurs, and you figuratively push the stop button on your personal remote control. It is as if time stands still for moments, and you can stand from afar and watch the event unfold. Secondly, you think, and begin to ask yourself several questions: Is this action going to help me or hurt me? Is this action in my best interest or will it work against me? Once you get those answers, you can become proactive and select a behavior, in other words, a response to the event and act on it. When it is over, then you press the rewind button to review what took place. Here you ask the ultimate question which is how did this all turn out? If all is favorable, another experience gained; if unfavorable, what adjustments do you have to make if confronted with a similar situation in the future? Can you make any tweaks to your response to the current situation that will shift things in a positive direction? This seems like a lot to accomplish in moments, how-ever, after much practice it does become automatic. Many of my students would put the card in their plan-ner, in the plastic covering of their binder, or in their wallets, anywhere that served as a reminder for them. It takes three weeks to make something a habit which means doing it every day, not just once in a while. It's like the old joke says, "How do you get to Carnegie Hall? Practice, Practice, Practice." S.T.A.R. as part of an individual's repertoire is exactly the same.

We all know that there are those students for whom school is difficult, challenging and/or not enjoy-able for whatever reason; maybe in fact that was you as a student. Now as a counselor, you are privileged to help your students navigate the obstacles in order to find their purpose, their meaning, and their joy. It starts by getting involved and finding the small pond within the ocean. Especially at a large high school, it can often seem daunting to discover how to become a name and not a number. "Finding one's mini-family" is finding a safe haven: those other adolescents who are like-minded and know the inside track. Whether it is band, sports, choir, art, drama, yearbook, journalism, photography, the associated student body, [and many more], they each have their own language, code of behavior, and a dimension of creativity. I used to love to watch as members of those areas related to each other. I vividly recall a freshman who was on the case-load of the counselor next door to me. Almost every day he would be in her office crying. He was so sad and seemed so lost. I would sometimes speak with him if he had to wait for her for some reason. One day they decided he would switch from PE to ROTC, and he became a different person. The tears stopped; the smiles came. One of the final activities of the school year that I always attended was the ROTC Awards Ceremony. It wasn't that I was a military-minded person [although the daughter of a Navy WWII Veteran], but I had so much respect for the commander and his team of instructors. They never tried to indoctrinate the students that a military career was what they should pursue; they only tried to teach good citizenship, leadership, and camaraderie, and they did it very well. During the ceremony, each student was called by name and their accomplishments and awards announced. Everyone was recognized. When his name was called and he walked across the stage, he was beaming. There was no trace of that sad, lonely young teenager; he was a confident, happy teenager thanks to his ROTC family, and a counselor who was there for him during those dark early days of high school.

So, how does a student find their home away from home? Here are my two sets of questions to aid you in helping your students navigate this journey; I call them my trilogies: A] Where was I? Where am I? Where am I going? and B] What am I doing? What do I want? Is what I am doing getting what I want? Those six questions will consume hours of discussion, dialogue, and discovery.

On the flip side of developing friendships, it is also important to know one's boundaries and limits in order to recognize what the student wants to avoid. Here enters the philosophy I referred to as "the crabs in the pot." I often asked a student who got into trouble if they knew how to cook crab. Sometimes I would get a look as if to say, "Is this really relevant Mrs. Regas," but they'd let me continue [it was after all my office!]. Most of the time they didn't know, and I'd say you put them in a pot of boiling water; then I would ask, "Why don't the crabs crawl out of the pot?" The answer is because the crabs on the bottom pull the top crabs down. Honestly, students got it right away. Misery does love company; so, if I can convince you to do something daring, risky, wrong, or to break the rules, then it validates my urge to do so and gives me a "partner in crime," as they say. The difficulty is when popularity becomes the deciding factor or being cool or accepted versus exercising one's conscience. The reality is this is an issue of integrity: sometimes standing for something means standing alone. This becomes monumental when it comes to stopping bullying. There are so few bullies compared with a large number of bystanders. If bystanders each removed themselves from the crowd mentality and stood alone against the injustice, bullies wouldn't stand a chance. It's like the late Justice Ruth Bader Ginsburg said: "Fight for the things that you care about but do it in a way that will lead others to join you." You see, one voice *can* start a chorus. If an individual doesn't have his/her integrity, who are they? What have they got? When you look yourself in the mirror, whom do you see and also want others to see? These are questions we must all ask ourselves throughout our entire lives as challenges come upon us. As a counselor, you can model this for your students while listening as they talk themselves through what can be a painful process.

Let's explore integrity a bit more and compare it to the concept of a team. The former references a characteristic in an individual, and the latter describes a group in which an individual claims membership. One differentiation is quickly identified in a single character, i.e., the letter "i" itself. The letter "i" is part of integrity while clearly missing in the word team. Integrity, one's virtue or principle, becomes a component of the team [company or troupe] the individual is a member. Without integrity, the individual team member lessens the strength of the group resulting in costly ramifications. Sadly, we are currently experiencing much of this in our country that has fractured us as a nation. It is an important reason why teaching, stressing, and modeling integrity is a vital role of the counselor. When the topic is addressed and not avoided, I believe it ultimately deepens the counselor/student relationship and will also leave a lasting impact.

Chapter 5

Establishing Parents As Your Allies

THE STUDENT IS your focus that *is* true. Nevertheless, the counselor/student dyad will actually be strengthened by developing a counselor/parent relationship. As a counselor, you will walk a fine line between a trusting rapport with each. Students need to know they can confide in you without the fear you are going to call their parent the minute they leave your office: this, of course, is outside the purview of being a mandated reporter and things that if you withheld from parents would be costly; simultaneously, parents need to know that you see their student as an individual and always have the best interest of their child/adolescent in your thoughts and actions. Years ago, I had a young man who was a senior and hadn't taken school as seriously as he was capable of doing; hence, he found himself deficient in his senior year and had to attend the after-school credit makeup program. Both his credits and grade point average were at stake. He and I spent a lot of time together with an exact plan laid out before him. Sadly, he and his mom weren't on the best terms and his lack of performance made things worse: obviously he was not following my "be your own best friend and not your own worst enemy" philosophy mentioned earlier. Although he was doing well in the after-school program, he received another F on his first progress report of the second semester. The clock was ticking. I received a phone call from his irate mother. She emphatically said if he did not improve immediately, she would take him out of the school and sign him up to prepare for and take the exam to earn his high school equivalency diploma [GED]. He and I had already discussed this as he had shared her demands with me. After letting her express herself, I reminded her that her son and I had been working closely together and that I met with him regularly and would continue to do so. I asked her to trust me and not ask her son anything about school because when they went up against each other, he shut down and faltered in school. I validated how painful this was for her, and I recognized her fear that he would not graduate from high school. I also acknowledged I knew as a parent myself what I was asking her to do. Since she and I had already built a relationship, she reluctantly agreed. I told her if she needed to talk, vent, and/or wanted someone who understood to listen, she could call me anytime. Her son and I met again with a revised plan. I explained to him her fears and that she was giving him a gift by backing off. I also asked him how badly he wanted to earn his diploma because no matter how much I wanted it for him [his mother as well], it wouldn't happen unless <u>he</u> wanted it more. [Note the rule of thumb, in counseling, never work harder than your students]. We made a deal. At the end of the year when the registrar reviews all credits and grade point averages to confirm graduates, his name was on the list. He had done it! As the semester progressed, his confidence grew, her stress lessened, and their relationship strengthened. I was thrilled when she called me to confirm his impending graduation. That is what a trusting relationship looks like and it doesn't happen randomly or suddenly; it is built, nurtured, groomed, and respected.

I had another young man who had an I.E.P. [Individualized Education Plan] since he had a learning disability. His parents were divorced, remarried, and it wasn't amicable at all. We had a meeting to discuss his behavior in school and some of his struggles. Different teachers stopped by and shared information; his case manager also attended and presented her perspective. Towards the end, it was just the student, two parents, two stepparents, and me. He and I were at opposite ends of the long table while the "Hatfields and the McCoys" sat opposite each other; trust me when I say, the pitchforks were flying. They began to argue and blame the other parent. I was watching my student, their son, melt into his chair. I politely interrupted them and asked the student to leave for a moment, with a promise to return when I invited him back in. He and I had a good relationship, so he knew I was protecting him, and he was thrilled to walk out for sure. I closed the door and sat back down. I leaned forward in my chair while I quietly and firmly told them what had just occurred would not continue under my watch. Despite claiming to care so much about their son, their behavior and words were hurting him. Unless they agreed to be calm and put their son's needs first, I would end the meeting without bringing him back in and strictly work with him and his teachers. I asked them to take a deep breath and ask themselves why they were there and how they imagined fighting was helping their son. Then I sat quietly for a few moments to let them ponder and give me their response. If I didn't have a relationship with them before this, one that assured them I was their son's advocate, I couldn't have proceeded as I did. Please know I didn't raise my voice. In fact, just so you know, my students learned early on in my career, that when I was upset with a student, my voice would actually lower. Learning to diffuse a situation is mandatory in being an effective counselor. Both parents apologized and said they wanted to continue; I thanked them and brought their son back into the room. Before he and I reentered the room,

I told him I was proud of him for staying calm, and I was sorry things got out of control: the parents' behavior confirmed what I frequently told students, i.e., adults don't always get things right. I assured him the rest of the meeting would be different [which it was]. He trusted me, and I never broke that trust. He didn't hesitate and walked back into the room. By the way, he too was a senior and graduated.

Although you are the student's counselor, sometimes parents need your advice, wisdom, compassion, and kindness. My open-door policy included parents being able to make appointments. If they showed up unannounced [which they often did], I would see them if I could. However, if speaking with the parent would shortchange a student, I would not hesitate to ask them to wait or offer to schedule an appointment. Students were <u>always my first priority</u>.

A combination that counselors have to handle is what I described as "the poison duo," i.e., entitled students and enabling parents. It magnifies any negative situation no matter how small it may seem. The student demands your attention [you have to see me now], an action [you have to write my letter of recommendation today], or a favor [get me out of this teacher's class so I can do better]. Each of those scenarios requires time and effort explaining why or why not; all delivered by a counselor exercising great patience. You think you have it under control, and then the unwelcome email, phone call, or appearance at your door occurs; no matter how delivered, the message is the same: you, as the counselor, are 1] not doing your job, 2] neglecting their son/daughter, and 3] consequently, negatively impacting their student's education. If that is not enough, the threat to go over your head is levied. Some days I used to say that my head hurt from so many people stepping on it! Breathing, staying calm, and having confidence in *your* decisions are crucial. You <u>have to</u> state your case as to what you did and why, and what you are more than willing and able to do. The latter has to be included so that both student and parent know that you, as the counselor, are truly invested in the student. It is difficult for any student to feel they don't matter to you and for any parent to believe their student is merely a number to you, not a name. So, the lessons for counselors are the same as for students, i.e., to act and not react.

Needless to say, relationships with students or parents have to be treated with respect, kid gloves [at times], and kindness; all persons must realize they matter to you. It's an art form, not a science and requires a great deal of effort. Just as no two students are the same, no two parents are either; one size does not fit all: stop, breathe, look, listen, assess, plan, and implement. If neglected for any reason, there is a price to pay. When trust is broken, it definitely takes *longer* to repair and rebuild.

Chapter 6

Relationships With Administrators And Teachers

AS MENTIONED EARLIER, counselors are the only ones in a school who have four entities to please all at once: students, parents, administration, and teachers, and as previously cited, they are not all on the same page simultaneously. I know that comes as quite a shock! It's as if you are juggling, and suddenly you find yourself with all four balls crashing down on you. While trying to appease *everyone*, someone steps on your head trying to get to a person with more authority because they don't like what you've said or done. They certainly don't teach you how to do this in school. Instead, the mantra is about achieving; we are all working for the common good synchronously!

Starting from the student as the focal point, it always amazed me that while adolescents crave independence, the right to make their own decisions, they flip the switch when it serves them to have someone else impose their will. To explain, I will use my all-time favorite scenario; seconds after an unhappy student left my office, almost like clockwork, the phone would ring; after stating my phone greeting, I would hear, "How come you told my daughter/son...?" [you can fill in the blank, but usually it had something to do with the word no]. It required me to listen to the entire speech, and then, politely respond by stating what I *really* said and the reason[s] why. Until I recalled the student back into my office, the situation was still ongoing. I had to explain the conversation I had with their parent, and why the vicious cycle should <u>immediately</u> cease and desist. This simply confirms the necessity and power of continually building and fostering relationships with <u>all</u> parties involved. Relationships are definitely *not* a one and done experience; they are continually evolving.

Teachers, on the other hand, often see their classrooms as islands. They build their world with their subject and their students. It is important to emphasize to students once they cross the threshold into a teacher's classroom, his/her rules hold; whether or not the student just came from a teacher who does things completely the opposite is irrelevant. It is often difficult for a student to wrestle with this concept, especially if one rule they like/deem fair and the other way not so much. As their counselor, you must begin to help them explore how to be a good citizen in a particular environment, whether they like it or not, and get their needs met. Therefore, when you are talking about a rule they despise, first, listen and validate them; then pull out one of your two power words, nevertheless or regardless. Your job is to help them be successful within that setting, not to debate nor to agree [even if you do] that the rule doesn't make sense.

Now we will focus on the teacher vs. the counselor. When a counselor receives a referral for an infraction by a particular student [by the way, it was my least favorite way of interacting with students, and I guarantee most counselors feel the same], how to handle that referral becomes the decision of the counselor. It becomes difficult when a teacher begins to tell you what punishment to levy. I had many conversations with only a few teachers [thank goodness] who thought they could dictate my response. A respectful conversation is necessary to clarify that relinquishing the referral to the counselor, also means trusting she/he will deal with the situation appropriately. To avoid situations like this, I would invite them to visit me [open door policy again] to discuss our roles and collaboration. First, I would ask them questions about the student's performance and their concerns; then, I would ask how I could support them. Having these discussions made the referral incidents much fewer and far between. The teacher felt heard, validated, and supported, and then we became a team working for the student's best interest. Those conversations and the camaraderie were priceless, as was the establishment of a mutual admiration society.

Since my husband was a teacher and then an administrator, I learned a lot from him about education before I entered the field. Private conversations are truly the best way to handle conflict as opposed to confronting someone with an audience. When students challenge a teacher in front of other students, the confrontation level is escalated. The teacher and the student become actors on a stage, and the class, now the audience, waits to see how the play will end. The teacher can't afford to lose the *entire* class, so it's an automatic loss for the student. When the student stays quiet and later asks the teacher if they can speak privately, after class or after school, the audience is no longer a factor; the conflict becomes one-on-one. This enables the teacher to focus on one student and one incident, which is far less threatening for either party. Hopefully, this results in a win/win situation. If the student tried unsuccessfully to do the above and notified me, I would contact the teacher and set up a meeting in my office with the three of us. The ground rules were as follows: 1] I facilitated each person telling their own story while never speaking for either party; 2] Each person was to listen without interruption; 3] We collaborated to create a positive resolution for both the student and the teacher. It always amazed me what each party [including me], learned about the other.

Since the buck stops at administration, depending on the administrator, there is often less negotiation. Private conversations and being able to use an "I statement" are still valuable. Learning this technique is a must in any form of communication. As humans, we tend to point the finger figuratively by using the word you: a] you made me mad, b] you did this, c] you said that, as a few examples. It creates a defensive receiver and what I call the ten-foot pole theory. It's as if there is a ten-foot pole between you and the other person, and every time the word "you" is spoken, it pushes the receiver away; the parties involved never get close to any resolution. When the word I is used, the receiver softens because she/he is hearing a story about the sender. No one knows you better than you do; therefore, I_____ tells the listener the message is about you, the sender, so it is safe for them to continue to listen. Here's a great phrase to practice and teach: I feel _____, when _____, because_____. I want _____. It is thoughtful, takes ownership, and expresses what is going on with the sender that the receiver may not know. Talking to teachers, administrators, parents, students, friends, spouses, whomever, we are never too old to learn and use good communication skills. I'd ask students to write out what they wanted to say to their teacher or their parents, practice it [with me if they chose], and then let me know what happened after they had the conversation. Definitely, the stress level and the anger subsided, allowing them to speak calmly and honestly. As counselors, we need to practice what we preach; using this tool may make it easier to speak with an administrator, teacher, or parent, especially if your working relationship is not a strong one.

Chapter 7

Skills Of Being A Successful Student: Counselor Taught & Reinforced

HOME IS THE first school where pride in achievement, internal rewards, and work ethic are all taught and modeled [positively or negatively]; sometimes it is deliberate and well thought out, and sometimes it is random without thought or care. Regardless, it all requires much effort. When organized school begins, the teacher becomes the person of influence. My oldest granddaughter used to tell her parents that her kindergarten teacher "didn't do it that way." Her teacher became the expert, the be-all and end-all. As students grow, they begin to develop their own personalities and ways of doing things. The extremes of the spectrum are reinforced or ignored. I remember a parent telling me when I called to discuss a behavior issue, "He's not my problem; he's with you all day." So, the reality is that schools are often expected to deliver everything with or without any support from home. By the time a student arrives in high school, habits [good or bad] are well established. Changing them will certainly be a challenge, and why assistance from the counselor is so necessary. Just like parents, teachers are different as well on how much time they focus on helping students be successful learners. Since the student has six teachers to manage, the counselor becomes the constant guiding force; hence, I decided to include this chapter. The following are the study skills I found many students had great difficulty executing; or worse yet, the skills were nonexistent. Therefore, a closer look is warranted at how to assist students in the development and implementation of these tools.

One of my favorites is the 10 Minute Rule for how long you study nightly: 10 times the grade you are in. Hence, a ninth grader should study an average of ninety minutes a night. Notice I say *average* because it will fluctuate, in length, depending on if anything is due the next day; nevertheless, studying nightly is a key to success. It is the thread that connects a student from day to day instead of starting over each day in class. It helps a student establish long term memory by using their brain as a filing cabinet. Each night when reviewing what they did in class, they are categorizing information for future retrieval. Then, by following that with preparations for the next day, the chain-link of knowledge is established. The next day in class, when a teacher refers to the preceding day, the student can recall what happened the previous night during their review and quickly regroup with the teacher rather than being confused or lost.

After reviewing what happened in each of their classes, a student can establish their to-do list for the evening. The use of a planner or agenda [hence referred to as planner] is very helpful to keep track of everything in one place. The planner becomes an integral tool. Having a planner out on the desk during class to jot down assignments, dates, and/or revisions quickly is beneficial. Frequently, I found students would wait until the end of class to pull out their planner, start to write down the assignment, and then the bell would ring; they were often late for their next class or left in a hurry with an incomplete assignment notation. At home, the planner can help a student prioritize assignments in order to complete the most important first.

Notetaking is another form of check and balance for students. Learning not to write down every word and how to discern what the teacher deems most important is essential; developing and utilizing one's own shorthand or abbreviations that the student will remember is also key in effective notetaking. Particularly in difficult subjects for the student, rewriting notes can be beneficial, and often helps a student discover what they still do not understand. Here's where parents can help. When working with a parent, encourage them not to ask their student if they have done their homework. That is a yes or no question eliciting one of three answers: yes, didn't have any, or did it in class. End of conversation. Rarely will a student who butts heads with his/her parents over school answer no! Teach parents to ask what students should actually ask themselves every night to keep from missing anything: What did you/I do in class today? What do you/I prepare for tomorrow? Remembering two questions is far easier to recall than trying to remember each lesson specifically. Now you and I both know that parents don't actually "need" to know about photosynthesis or the Pythagorean theorem, but if a student can't explain something in a way that makes sense to the listener, they know there is a gap. Saying something out loud creates what I referenced as an "auditory-motor loop," which means you say the words, hear the words, comprehend the words, and then move on. Sometimes [and we've all been there], you're talking and think, "That doesn't make any sense at all." Parents then become a sounding board [win/win for both parties] instead of a drill sergeant [which makes both parents and their student agitated and exhausted].

Another trilogy I developed [yes, I like things that come in threes] is my 3 Alls to Success: Do All of the work, All of the time, and Always turn it in! When I would review grades with students who were flailing and saw lots of zeros, the red flag revealed itself. I was always amazed at students who were unaware of missing assignments or that a zero impacted their grades dramatically. The 3 Alls erase all censorship that students often make unconsciously: "I only do the work I like; I only do the work for the teacher I like; I don't work on my birthday, on Mondays, on Fridays; I forget to turn things in." Any one of those single-handedly will spell disaster for the student. The 3 Alls take the thought process out and revert to, you guessed it, Nike!

Active listening is imperative as a tool in learning how to ask questions. There are four steps: hearing, clarifying, understanding, responding. Students would say to me, "Well, I just don't get it," and I would reply, "What does that really mean?" Students jump from hearing to responding, and there are no shortcuts in the process of listening which is why it is called active. When a hand is raised, and a teacher hears I don't get it or I don't understand, a teacher may think the student wasn't listening; the teacher often repeats it exactly as they did originally [after all, it makes sense to them]. In reality, the student may actually need to hear it twice to process the information. However, if a student reframes the question by describing what they heard, and where in the explanation they got lost, it draws a map for the teacher. She/he now knows where the student took a detour, and then can rephrase the answer or commentary from a different direction. This simple technique helps reveal what the student heard and is not confrontational or a waste of time; it tells the teacher they definitely want to learn the material, and categorically, that is what the teacher wants. It truly is a win/win situation!

Test-taking is often a source of great stress for students. Anxiety can make it very difficult to focus and relax; it is necessary to diminish stress to allow the information learned to be remembered and critical thinking to be utilized. When a student and I discussed test-taking, I would ask them their process in actually taking a test. A common thing I discovered was that many students scan the entire test. Hearing their stories, I realized as we scan, our eye catches words, phrases, formulas which trigger a response; often, it creates a new problem where all of the information starts converging and thereby gets mixed up. As you recall, the first step in S.T.A.R. is to stop and slow things down. Students have to learn how to apply this technique to test-taking. After writing their name/date on the test, I instructed students to take one question at a time. There are three types of questions: 1] I've got this; 2] I'm pretty sure I know this, but it will take a bit more effort; 3] I have no clue. The key is to skip the #3s and do all of the #1s and #2s, solidifying the student's confidence. When that is completed, then go back and do all of the #3s. If necessary, i.e., they are easily distracted, a student can ask the teacher if it is all right for them to use a blank sheet of paper to cover the test except the question they are working on; this can be especially helpful during math tests. When students put this into practice, they feel they are gaining time instead of running out of time. Besides using these techniques, students should do three more things: 1] get an adequate night of sleep, 2] eat a good breakfast, and 3] avoid cramming which adds to stress. Studying nightly is the best anecdote for the latter.

Flashcards are a standard tool, which I believe doesn't go out of style. The problem with flashcards is when the rubber band breaks, they fall all over the place. A solution for that is to punch a hole in the corner of each card and get a metal ring to attach them. A student can flip them over and over for a quick review on the bus, in the car, or as a nightly review. Two weeks before graduation, counselors at the high school I was at were given name cards for their seniors. After meeting with each senior to assure the correct pronunciation, I would take the cards home and every night, say the names out loud. Those were my "flashcards," so I did practice what I preached.

If a teacher uses a textbook in their class, students must learn how to read it; this way, students will glean the most information. First, always go to the end of the chapter to see the questions asked; this way the reader knows, in advance, what the author deems important. Second, go to the start of the chapter and read each heading and everything in bold. Lastly, return to the beginning and read the complete chapter.

The puzzle is much clearer with this methodology, and the reading takes on a deeper meaning. Applying the principle of gleaning information when listening to the teacher is also vital. This includes what they write on the board, what they repeat or say in multiple ways, and referencing study guides they may produce; they all become the tools to discern what material the teacher deems the most important.

Finally, there are two kinds of 3 Rs in education. The one that's been around all of my years is "Reading, 'Riting, and 'Rithmetic." We know that it all needs to be wrapped in critical thinking to get the most out of it. There is, however, an emotional 3 Rs: Respect for self, Respect for others, and Responsibility for one's actions. Together these six things make education empowering for the learner and will carry them through life. Sometime in the late '90s, I recall hearing the results of a study shared on the national news. It emphatically said, no matter what a student's college major, if they graduated with leadership, communication, and collaboration skills, they would be successful. I believe, as a counselor, the goal is to help our students gain those skills in collaboration with the concepts in this chapter.

Chapter 8

COVID And What It Has Done To Education

WHEN I STARTED this project in early 2020, COVID was not in the picture. Now it dominates every aspect of our existence, our daily living, and <u>nothing</u> escapes its reign of terror and confusion. I think about my former colleagues a lot and know so much is weighing on them. I have to say that politics has no place in education or healthcare. We need a literate, healthy populous to survive as a nation. *No one* should be shortchanged because of where they live, their race or ethnicity, who their community leaders are, or who heads the nation. It is a no brainer to me that education and healthcare should permanently become national/regional/local priorities; and that is the period and end of the sentence!

It was an incredible experience for my husband and me to watch our granddaughters from afar [we live on opposite coasts] handle the challenges of online learning. Let's examine the positives first. We live in a highly intense technological era. What I have to work at is second nature to my granddaughters. If this had occurred twenty, even ten years ago, the story would be very different. Ensuring each student had access to a computer was a task the school district I worked for focused on first. Of course, this is the equity factor and had [and still has] to be addressed. Teachers, like students and parents, are at different skill levels as well. Their challenges were enormous. Then it had to be put all together, so it made sense to everyone, and students still knew they had a teacher or teachers who cared about them. Last spring, I was deeply moved to see the connections made via the "drive-by," along with virtual graduations and promotions. Little details that truly made a difference. As the saying goes, "it takes a village," which means everyone has to help out. We became our first-grade granddaughter's reading partners; every morning we gathered through "What's App" to connect, listen, help, guide, and encourage her efforts. It was important for us [as retired educators] to focus her thoughts on the process; it was very different, but it was *still* school. In my mind, when the school year ended, the next step would have been to spend the summer evaluating what happened in the spring and how to make it better in the fall. I believe we lost valuable time going back and forth between reopening/hybrid/online models, something like putting the "cart before the horse," as they say. The push from certain leaders that schools MUST reopen in the fall caused me to be deeply saddened [and I still am] by two things: 1] there was no talk of increasing the funding to make all of the necessary alterations to what we know as school, and 2] I never heard counselor mentioned in any context. I heard about the safety/well-being of the students, teachers, cafeteria workers, custodians, office staff, and bus drivers, each specifically named. I totally agree as *everyone* matters, but where were the counselors in all of this? As a counselor who used to run support groups, I know the benefits they provide to students. [I had 10 running weekly and different counselors, school psychologists, and teachers worked with me in co-facilitating them; if possible, it's beneficial to have two facilitators per group]. I loved facilitating groups. Oddly, my favorite group [I facilitated it all eighteen years I was at the school] was the grief group. I would tell students it is the group you love to belong to but hate the reason why because it meant you lost someone you loved. Sometimes it is losing something [a job, a friendship, or in this case... school as we knew it]. The grief group was the most welcoming, accepting group year after year. A group to help students deal with their losses and anxiety would be most appropriate now to cope with all of the uncertainty the pandemic has unleashed. During our grief groups, we didn't talk about death exclusively. We talked about life, how to move forward, how to handle the anniversaries and holidays without that person; it was a place to go and be quiet or share and be safe either way. I had students who participated in a group all four years of high school. It was a lifeline for them. The feelings of grief can suddenly and unexpectedly consume a person. Despite everything appearing fine on the outside, on the inside, the person is overwhelmed by grief. To illustrate this, I would tell my personal story. My mother, who was my best friend other than my husband, had died during my first year in the district. She didn't drive. One day I was driving down a road between our homes, and I saw a petite silver-haired woman waiting at the bus stop. It was as if someone had just punched me in the stomach. I saw my mother in the woman's image. Tears welled up in my eyes and I gasped aloud. I slowed down, took a deep breath, and composed myself. That is the roller coaster of grief. The general school [classmates and others] may not understand what you are feeling or why, but your fellow group members do. I was always surprised at the number of schools that didn't offer support groups. Now with COVID and the sense of disconnection, I believe groups are even more vital. ZOOM, another phenomenon of our time, is a perfect way to conduct a group online. The rules of a group stand and should be reviewed at the start of each group meeting; here are a few I used: 1] what is said in group, stays in group [although a counselor must notify students that she/he is a mandated reporter if someone is hurting themselves, hurting someone else, or someone is hurting them]; 2] no name-calling, put-downs to self or others; 3] no interruptions; 4] come to group sober; 5] be punctual; 6] respect every member of the group; 7] everyone has the right to talk or to pass; 8] even if a student passes and stays silent, listening and engagement in the group is expected; 9] use "I" statements while not talking about others; 10] no side conversations. A support group is <u>not</u> therapy; it is a chance to be in a safe place, have someone who listens, who cares, and a chance to explore one's feelings. Opportunities like this make a difference, especially during these unprecedented times. They are crucial to the emotional success of students, and ultimately their academic success. It will also be the bridge between "the school" we knew and "the school" we are creating.

Many years ago, our district had a superintendent who believed online learning was a necessity for everyone. The district adopted a program where students could make up missing credits through an online program. Since online learning is no longer a novelty but is now the norm, I find it fascinating to hear the repetitive declaration that it is not the same or as good as in-person instruction. I absolutely agree, but I don't believe it has ever been as good or a substitute. Sometimes we don't know what we had until we've lost it. I hope this will be a lesson learned so that when we move past COVID, we as a society will invest in public education like never before. In the meantime, I suggest districts throughout this country engage retired educators to volunteer an hour weekly to tutor students or counselors to conduct support groups. It would be a source of comfort for students, parents, and teachers. Currently, it *remains* an untapped resource, thus, a loss for everyone.

Chapter 9

How To Transition To and Through High School

HIGH SCHOOL IS the last four years of one's mandatory education, public or private; graduation is the pinnacle of milestones because it is the culmination of thirteen years of an individual's life. There is no other milestone quite like it because in this movie, "the star" moves through childhood, preteen, teens, and finally arrives at adulthood. Now, we all realize that turning eighteen is nothing magical: no bells, no whistles, no makeover; however, the law begins to treat an eighteen-year-old differently because they have crossed over the precipice into the final chapter of evolution, i.e., coming of age. In reality, this chapter usually lasts several decades longer than any other developmental stage; however, according to the law, an eighteen-year-old is treated the same as someone twenty-five, fifty, or seventy-five years of age. Students have to be cognizant of that.

High school is a microcosm of the world outside. It is why I stressed the importance of knowing what school is *really* about, i.e., Chapter 3; it is also why those "seven characteristics" should not be taken lightly. When I would speak with eighth-grade students about preparing to come to high school in the fall, I would emphasize to them [and their parents when I spoke at parent meetings], how to focus each year.

Ninth grade is the introduction. It is the student's responsibility to explore the campus to learn where things are, where key people are, and where resources are located. First and foremost [yes, I am biased], introduce yourself to your counselor! Remember, "Be nice to your counselor...she/he writes your recommendations." The student must realize there is only one of them while their counselor has a caseload of most likely anywhere from 250 to 500 students; depending on the school, it could actually be even more or less; my average was between 450 and 525, but sadly, one year I actually had a caseload of 650 students. The more times the student visits the counselor, the better the counselor will get to know them. I was always so impressed with freshmen who took the time to visit me, ask questions, and share their thoughts and ideas; they already had an idea of what they wanted from high school. With each visit, it was easy to see their comfort and confidence levels rise. On the other hand, I was saddened when a student came wandering into the counseling office asking to speak to his/her counselor. If I replied, I would ask the name of their counselor. When I got the answer, "I don't know," I had to seize the teachable moment.

Also imperative in ninth grade is putting into practice the 10 Minute Rule, the P.A.N.T.S. tool, and the other study tools previously discussed. In addition, freshman year is where students start to clearly define their likes and dislikes while expressing their personality in their own unique fashion.

One other philosophy that is also good to establish during the freshmen year is what I refer to as "challenge with balance." More is often deemed better in our society; hence, if one advanced class is good, two are definitely better, and several honors and/or advanced placement [AP] classes would be best. A <u>student</u> holds the scale. I always told students I wanted them to challenge themselves but not drown. A college or university in examining a prospective student's transcript will look at their trajectory throughout high school: did they challenge themselves a bit more each year? Some students can handle taking four AP courses concurrently, while for others, taking one advanced course is their best challenge. A student mustn't skate through high school by making little to no effort. It's just as important they don't take on too much, so they feel as if they are drowning. This level of stress can potentially make them emotionally and/or physically ill. Colleges don't look favorably on the student who took the easy road, nor on the student that overloads, does poorly, and proceeds to drop several advanced classes. Both demonstrate mismanagement.

Tenth grade is what I used to call the free year; it isn't free academically [because every year matters] but it is free in the sense the student doesn't have to make any decisions. Now is the time to delineate the following: "I like this, I don't like that; I'm interested in this while that bores me; I have no clue about this, but I want to know more." It's analogous to laying steppingstones which will ultimately create a pathway towards a post-secondary choice. Sophomore year, in October, is also the time to take the PSAT exam. It's not just taking the exam that matters, but what you do with the results. It used to amaze and disappoint me when we had hundreds of exams never picked up, and they had to be delivered to classrooms. It was equally frustrating when students would pick up their exams, review their scores, and then toss everything. The scores don't teach you anything that leads to growth. The PSAT is the only exam that returns the test booklet with an explanatory printout to test-takers. The explanation tells students the correct answers and their answers, so they know exactly where they struggled. Since students have the test, they can return to the question and think, "This is my answer, this is the right answer; where did my thought process go awry?" If there are lots of zeros at the end, students know they ran out of time. Remembering the three types of test questions, they probably could have captured more correct answers if they had initially skipped the I don't know questions. The results also break down the types of questions, i.e., algebra, geometry, reading, vocabulary, and lets them know how successful they were in each category. If students truly analyze and study their results, the PSAT becomes the best prep for taking the SATs: in the spring of their junior year and the fall of their senior year. [Note, even though COVID has halted these types of exams, I suspect someday they will return].

Upon entering their junior year, the student is halfway through high school and is now considered an upperclassman. First, they should take the PSAT even if they took it as a sophomore, as national merit scholarships are awarded to qualifying juniors. Also, this is the year to start exploring colleges seriously. Encourage your students to take advantage of the wealth of knowledge college representatives bring to the campus. It will allow them to listen and learn what colleges are looking for and see what rings true for them as a student. Have them start making three lists: I must have this in a school; I would like to have this at a school; I don't care if it is at a school. If done thoroughly and diligently, a student starting their senior year should end up with six to ten colleges, each having all of the things they are interested in.

If you want to spark interest and concentration on the college application process, never ask your student what they want to be when they grow up or what they want to major in. The first question is ridiculous as most individuals change their minds several times before settling on something. The second question is difficult for many adolescents who have a variety of interests. Instead, ask the poignant questions, "What are you passionate about?" and "What are you truly interested in?" Those questions will open the door to self-exploration. Then, the student is less likely to answer by claiming a popular major or a trendy career. After this discussion, ask the follow-up questions: why does a particular school interest or intrigue them, and why can they see themselves on that campus. If they do state they want to major in a particular subject, make sure you ask them why; their responses will reveal how much they have researched the major and its requirements, and finally, where it may lead. When I asked those questions of a particular student, he stated he wanted to major in English; however, he expressed no enthusiasm or passion regarding it as a profession. So, I asked him, "What are you really interested in, and what do you really want to pursue?" He smiled and said, "Music, but I don't know what I could do with it." I had a wonderful brochure from a university on well over 100 careers in music. Suddenly, there was a smile on his face and excitement in his voice. He was going to a college representative's presentation that afternoon, and now he knew what he wanted to ask. He found a pathway that fit him.

Through these discoveries, a student will move towards applying to the right schools for the right reasons. Remind them that college is a time of discovery, so starting college with an undeclared major is all right. Especially for large universities, it is quite difficult to declare a major and then change directions midstream. In doing so, students may lose credits resulting in more time and money [to the dismay of parents] needed to graduate. Some students believe if they select a particular major, they will have a better chance of getting accepted by a college or university. Stress to your students there is no guarantee that will occur, and to remember it *may* be very costly switching majors. With an application, a student doesn't know the "pool" they are jumping into and what a particular college or university is looking for; the applicant doesn't know which college seniors are graduating, what spaces they are vacating, and what the institution is looking to fill. Students need to focus on being the best version of themselves and to be true to themselves. That said, there is more flexibility at small liberal arts colleges. One such school, Albion College, students don't have to declare a major until the end of their sophomore year and can still graduate in four years. Word to the wise, emphasize to your students they need to know the rules, regulations, and expectations of their chosen schools. Despite all of this, I realize a good portion of students [not the majority] know what they want to pursue, including their end goal. One such student graciously wrote the foreword of my book. From the first time I met her as a freshman, she said she wanted to be a doctor, and she never wavered throughout high school or college. Her determination, perseverance, and accomplishments have left me awestruck. I am very proud to still have her in my life.

With a foundation now established, make sure you stress, multiple times, the importance of not wasting an application, time or money, by applying to schools they have no intention of attending. I had a student who applied to twenty-eight schools unbeknownst to me. I received an email from several universities reminding me I had not submitted my counselor review of the student or my recommendation. I immediately sent for the student. When I inquired about the various schools and their letters to me, he flippantly stated he didn't want to go to most of the schools I cited; he merely applied to see if he could get in because they had no application fee. I explained how disrespectful that was to the universities because it took time away from reviewing an application from someone who really wanted a spot on their campus. It was also disrespectful to me since we had met several times about the application process and selection, and he never mentioned his laundry list of applications. As a counselor, I took pride in responding to emails, phone calls, and letters with expediency. In the eyes of the college, I was not complying with their requirements. For the first time, he understood the gravity of the situation. I explained that he needed to write to every school he had no intention of attending, whether accepted or not; it was respectful to thank them for their time, but he had changed his mind and was no longer interested in pursuing their institution of higher learning.

Another decision that backfired for a student dealt with Early Action [EA] vs. Early Decision [ED]. As a counselor, I never recommended a student opt for Early Decision as this is binding; in other words, if the college accepts the student, they are committed to attending: the college says, jump, and the student says how high. In my career, I had very few students that unequivocally knew if they received a letter of congratulations as a result of an ED application, they would gladly and willingly submit a Statement of Intent to Register, i.e., S.I.R. The majority of students, however, do not have a strong level of attachment to one school. Hence, they still want to be able to weigh their options and compare financial packages. One of my former students decided to apply to an Ivy League school and opted for Early Decision. I had a full discussion with him regarding what binding actually meant and tried to help him determine if he and his parents fully agreed with the terms of Early Decision [since finances are involved]. Even though he couldn't honestly rule out his desire for a few other schools, he wanted the prestige of Early Decision. Early Action, on the other hand, means you get a ruling by the institution before non-Early Action applicants, i.e., Regular Decision students. However, you don't have to commit to the school immediately. You can wait and submit your decision on May 1st, the regular deadline date. Lo and behold, I received a letter from this prestigious university stating my name was on the recommendation letter for this young man. The school had accepted his ED application, and he was to respond within ten days; he did not comply with the ED agreement. The letter continued with the rescind- ment of his acceptance. Additionally, he could never apply to the institution again. The Dean of Admissions signed the letter. Needless to say, I was stunned and angry. I immediately wrote a letter of apology stat- ing I had advised against ED and was not aware the student had gone ahead anyway. The student had not even notified me of his acceptance. I explained that my signature is my integrity. I hoped if they received a letter of recommendation from me in the future, they would take it seriously as I do not write anything I do not mean. After getting the letter into the mail, I sent a pass out to the student's classroom. When he came to my office, I showed him the letter. He was stunned and embarrassed. I also called his parents with him in my office so he could hear my end of the conversation. By the way, that can be an important tool if you are work- ing with a student who tends to tell half-truths to his/ her parents; the call becomes your check and balance. I suggested to both the student and the parents he should write a letter of apology to the university. This is a clear and excellent example of how sometimes despite your best efforts, students will make decisions that do not serve them well. Follow up by you as the counselor is crucial. Your name is referenced, and your professional reputation and integrity under scrutiny.

Finally, encourage your students to go to college fairs, take virtual tours, correspond with college representatives, and discuss with their parents their reasons for wanting to go out of state or not. After I retired, I became a part-time regional representative for an out of state private college. I became part of a group known as RACC, Regional Admission Counselors of California. They lived in California but represented schools outside of the state. These men and women, full-time regional admissions counselors, gave so much to students. They were always traveling to ensure they saw as many students as possible: four to five school visits/fairs plus student interviews via the phone or in-person was a typical day. They held nothing back. Their expertise should not be missed or taken lightly by students or by high schools. Their presence is a gift and should be appreciated. Invite your student[s] to visit you after attending a college fair or visiting with a college representative on your campus; this will help them process what they discovered about the institution[s] and how they will utilize their newfound knowledge. The more a student dialogues, the clearer things will become for them. As a counselor, you are the sounding board for your student. As they share their discoveries, the clarifying questions you ask will assist the student in understanding their journey. The appropriate and timely question can reveal a lot to a student: "How did you reach that decision?" "Why does that matter to you?" "Can you visualize yourself on that campus?" "What is your gut telling you about that school?" These are *not* yes/no questions; therefore, they cannot be answered off-the-cuff. These questions lead to lengthy discussions, and hopefully, the next level of research for the student. Remember, students are not providing you answers because *you* need to know but because *they* need to know; in telling you, they have told themselves. Hearing themselves is believing and confirming. It can also be the revelation that their decision doesn't make sense and the school in question is not the right place for them. Being a student's sounding board is powerful indeed. Here are two of my students on opposite ends of the process. I clearly recall a young woman coming into my office early in her senior year with a blue acrylic accordion folder with several pockets. In each pocket, she had information about a specific college or university she was exploring. She asked if we could discuss a particular school at each visit. Throughout the process, she would take notes and further define her rank order. She clearly identified her top school down to her least favorite, and surprisingly, sometimes they changed places. In the end, she knew exactly why she was applying to each school, which schools she ultimately eliminated, and the ones which amazed her and rose to the top of the list. Contrast that with a young man who stood in my doorway in March of his senior year declaring he had been accepted to three top colleges. I congratulated him and asked if he knew which school he was going to choose; his reply stunned and saddened me: "None of them." When I inquired why, he said, "Because I don't like any of them." He didn't do his research and applied to the schools for the wrong reasons. She, on the other hand, made the most of the entire application process. It made her final decision easy, clear, and joyous.

There's a wonderful book that I always recommended to juniors and seniors: <u>Choose the Right College and Get Accepted.</u> I liked the book because it is students telling their stories of what worked and what didn't. It is timeless. It's also an easy read and one where students can imagine themselves in the stories told in an inspirational way. The book is also near and dear to me because on page 101 is my oldest daughter's story. When she was in graduate school at NYU, the authors were writing the book and interviewed her. The book was a surprise Christmas present. Although that was my favorite page, I did assure students and parents I had read the book [it was highlighted throughout as proof], and honestly, I wouldn't recommend it if I didn't believe it would help them in their process.

All of this really can be capsulated in one of my favorite expressions, which I first used when I taught parenting: "I did the best I knew how at the time." It makes room for changing one's mind based on new information, new circumstances, discovered preferences, maturity, yet always moving forward. It takes away from the "could of/would of/should of" way of thinking that diminishes one's self-efficacy and holds an individual back. It is important to remember that life is made up of the past, the present, and the future. What stands between the present and the past is guilt, and what stands between the present and the future is worry. Both guilt and worry take an individual on a roller coaster ride going up and down and all around yet dropping them off exactly where they began. The present is the only thing we can impact; we can't change the past, and the future hasn't happened, so what's left is the here and now. If we miss it by predominantly hanging back or dreaming forward, we will miss amazing opportunities right here, right now. As counselors, our job is to help our students navigate their high school experience. This will help them glean everything they can in preparation for adulthood.

Throughout high school, there is one definitive conversation that needs to occur with students, especially seniors. During the thirteen years of school, a student's life is programmed from September to June, Monday through Friday, culminating in graduation. The day after graduation, shockingly to some, nothing happens UNLESS the student makes it happen. There are eight options after graduation: 1] get a job; 2] join the military; 3] enroll in a certification program; 4] attend a trade or technical school; 5] attend a community college to earn an Associate's Degree; 6] attend a community college and then transfer to a four-year university; 7] attend a four-year college or university; 8] do nothing [yes, it is an option although not a favorable one especially for parents]. One size does not fit all. Counselors have to assist students in exploring <u>all</u> of their options; they must also help them learn how to make the best decisions for themselves. We all have choices, and if we don't exercise them, we may end up in a place we don't know how we got there or didn't want to go. In conclusion, the aphorism deserves repeating: "I did the best I knew how at the time."

Chapter 10

Let Person-First Language Be Your Guide

I FIRST LEARNED that phrase when I was getting my pupil personnel credential. It penetrated me so personally. My youngest daughter was born two months preterm. She was often referred to [not by her father or me] as a "preemie." I loathed that description because it was always said in a tone of less than. I reframed it to preterm, which described when she was born but said nothing about her [she, by the way, was more than not less than]. I corrected people [politely, of course], and I taught others to use the term when I was a perinatal educator; this started in 1979 when she was born and carried throughout the 1980s and into the early 1990s. Fast forward to 1998, when I heard the phrase person-first language used during a class I was taking for my credential. All those years, that's how I was speaking, and now it had a label. It is imperative to use person-first language as a counselor. Education has many acronyms: 504s, IEPs, SPED, GATE, to name a few. We use them for quick identification and categorization, but when we use them to label students, we do them a disservice because we pigeon-hole them and often make assumptions. We must see each student as a unique individual and recognize we all have special needs one way or another. I recall a very intelligent young man I had the privilege of counseling. At the time, he had the diagnosis of Asperger's, which today is referred to as Autism spectrum disorder. He had a 504 plan which gave him specific accommodations to meet his needs. We were having his annual meeting in the main office conference room, and he and I were sitting opposite each other across the long table; on the sides were his teachers and his mothers. Before meetings like this, I always explained the process to the student; this way they understood the meeting would be conducted with them and for them, not at them or about them. They are a participant not a spectator. I wanted to lessen their anxiety and emphasize their value to the team. After I introduced the meeting and the agenda, I asked him if he would explain to everyone what he had shared with me about how he learns. I smiled at him and nodded for him to begin. He was so articulate and captivated everyone. You literally could hear a pin drop. He began with, "My brain works differently than yours does." Then he proceeded to elaborate and define in detail what that actually meant for him, what truly helped him learn in *every* class, while he addressed <u>each</u> teacher with specifics; not every subject required the same tools. Tears welled up in my eyes as I was so struck by his candor and his ability to ask for what he needed. He explained all he wanted was the chance to have the same opportunities as his classmates: basically, he asked to have the playing field leveled. He didn't want to be viewed as a demanding or difficult student, which before that moment, some of his teachers did. My job was to create a safe environment for him to express himself; then create a plan to help him achieve his goals.

This is a perfect example of the importance of helping students recognize their strengths, as well as, develop and utilize them. When I was a marriage and family therapist, I trained to use the Strength Deployment Inventory. What I loved about the tool was the concept of defining strengths and overdone strengths vs. strengths and weaknesses. No one likes to claim weaknesses; no one likes to view themselves as less than. It is helpful to recognize our strengths and learn how to develop them; however, we need to know when we overdo our strengths, we put ourselves at risk. For instance, if I have the strength of being trusting but overdo it, I become gullible and may fall for anything without testing its credibility. If I take my strength of having a solid work ethic and overdo it, it makes me less collaborative and/or makes me a workaholic with little or no time to rest: for example, I have to do it all myself, or it won't get done, or maybe it will get done, but not well. This way we begin to recognize when we are stretching the rubber band too far and can catch ourselves before it snaps back and stings us. So, for your students with needs that require more of your time and effort, don't define them by what we often designate as a disability. Instead, help them discover how they are "differently-able" and can apply those skills to learning. Once you see the whole picture, you will no longer be comfortable referring to students with labels: Special Ed, Jock, GATE, etc. You will refer to them by their first name, which will conjure up a list of characteristics. Don't compartmentalize your students; that's an automatic lose/lose. Person-first language says, "I see all of you." One other application of person-first language has to do with working with families. At the high school I worked at, I was fortunate as counselor caseloads were divided alphabetically using last names instead of grade-level counseling. I believe it is the preferred and most effective way of division as it allows a counselor to grow with his/her students. Grade-level counseling can compartmentalize you and your students, as you judge everything by the grade level you're assigned to; you have nothing to compare it to since you are not working with other grade levels. I believe working with alphabet-based caseloads keeps you sharper as a counselor. You are less likely to fall prey to performing robotically and repetitively, thereby treating "all freshmen" or whatever grade level the same way. As a counselor, you have to be on your toes as you constantly flip from one grade level to another since each has its own set of characteristics. Alphabet-based caseloads also give you four years to develop a relationship. The longer you work with a student, the better you get to know them. It's truly a privilege to watch them grow up during their last four years of education before entering the adult world. The better you know them, the more you can individualize your interactions with them; when you do that, the more they will trust you. Hence, you become a better counselor, and they can evolve more as a student. Working with a particular part of the alphabet adds another dimension; the counselor will most likely come across multiple students within the same family. You develop a relationship with the students within the family and the family unit as well. When a "new" family member came on board, I would always have this poignant conversation with the freshman. I would promise them I would not compare them to their sibling[s] but would view them as a unique individual. Secondly, I promised to never discuss them with their sibling[s], nor discuss their sibling[s] with them. Each student had the right to confidentiality with me. Finally, I promised I would never use siblings as messengers one to another: for example, "Please tell your brother to come and see me" or "Will you give this to your sister?" I always found those rules when *not* followed to be disrespectful to the student. Since respect was a prominent theme in my office, it was important for me to practice what I preached. When we had this conversation, I always found the student breathed a sigh of relief, body posture relaxed, and the conversation came more freely. They had been seen and validated as an important part of my caseload and not just lumped together as part of a clan. It truly strengthened our relationship from the start. You've heard the expression "teachable moment," well, this is a definite "relationship moment." Don't miss them!

Chapter 11

Some Of My Favorite Aphorisms

I COULDN'T END this narrative without sharing some of the many sayings that were pinned to my walls. Each day I was surrounded with messages which defined me to all who entered my office; these words soothed my soul, brought a smile to my face, granted me a quiet moment of serenity, and made that small space my home away from home. It also provided easily accessible teachable moments, catalysts for thought and discussion between me and my students. Depending on the conversation at hand, I would point to something and ask my student to read it out loud. Then after a bit, I would frame the conversation towards the epiphany I was hoping would transpire for that particular student. Sometimes I would see a student enter my office, just sit down, and gaze around the room. When their eyes seemed to stay focused on something, I would follow their lead by asking what was speaking to them. Those are some of my fondest memories.

They are in no particular order; some will have an author's name, and some will say unknown author. They are all sacred to me, and I hope they touch you in some small way.

1] "Courage means doing what is right even when you are afraid; it is not that you don't have fear." Unknown Author

2] "Coincidence is a miracle where God chooses to remain anonymous." Unknown Author

3] "The important thing in life is not so much where we are but in what direction we are moving." Oliver Wendell Holmes

4] "There is no progress without some discontent and discomfort." Unknown Author

5] "There is a sacredness in tears. They are not the mark of weakness but of power. They speak more eloquently than 10,000 tongues. They are messengers of overwhelming grief...and unspeakable love." Washington Irving

6] "Success is to be measured not so much by the position that one has reached in life as by the obstacles which one has overcome while trying to succeed." Booker T. Washington

7] "What is popular is not always right! What is right is not always popular!" Unknown Author

8] "Three things in life that can destroy a person... anger, pride & unforgiveness." Unknown Author

9] "Three things in life that you should never lose... hope, peace, honesty." Unknown Author

10] "The greater discovery is that a human being can alter his life by altering his attitude of mind." William James

11] "We must learn together as brothers or perish together as fools." Martin Luther King Jr.

12] "Hold on to what is good, even if it is a handful of earth. Hold on to what you believe, even if it is a tree that stands by itself. Hold on to what you must do, even if it is a long way from here. Hold on to life, even if it is easier to let go. Hold on to my hand, even if I have gone away from you." A Pueblo Blessing

13] "If there is anyone out there who still doubts that America is a place where all things are possible; who still wonders if the dream of our founders is alive in our time; who still questions the power of our democracy, tonight is your answer."

President-Elect, Barack Obama, 11/4/08

14] "What we do speaks so loudly to our children that when we talk, they cannot hear us." Unknown Author

15] "Be the difference you wish in this world." Mahatma Gandhi

16] <u>The Tale of Two Wolves</u>: One evening, an old Cherokee told his grandson about a battle that goes on inside people. He said, "My son, the battle is between two wolves inside each of us." One is evil. It is angry, envy, sorrow, regret, greed, arrogance, self-pity, guilt, resentment, inferiority, lies, false pride, superiority, and ego. The other is good. It is joy, peace, love, hope, serenity, humility, kindness, benevolence, empathy, generosity, truth, compassion, and faith." The grandson thought about it for a minute and then asked his grandfather, "Which wolf wins?" The old Cherokee simply replied, "The one you feed." Cherokee Wisdom

17] Fully Rely On God-F.R.O.G. Unknown Author

18] "The highest reward for a person's toil is not what they get for it, but what they become from it." Unknown Author

19] <u>For doing the Impossible.</u> "According to the theory of aerodynamics, as may be readily demonstrated through wind tunnel experiments, the bumblebee is unable to fly. This is because the size, weight, and shape of its body-in relation to total wingspan-make flying impossible. But the bumble-bee, being ignorant of these scientific truths, goes ahead and flies anyway, and makes a little honey on the side each day." The Master Teacher, Inc.

20] The world says, "Seeing is Believing." Faith says, "Believing is Seeing." Unknown Author

21] People may doubt what you SAY, but they will always BELIEVE what you do! Unknown Author

22] Last but not least, "A Little Story." Unknown Author

Once upon a time, there were 4 people named Everybody, Somebody, Anybody, and Nobody. There was an important job to be done, and Everybody was sure that Somebody would do it, but Nobody did it! Somebody got angry because it was Everybody's job. Everybody thought Anybody could do it, but Nobody realized that Everybody wouldn't do it. It ended up that Everybody blamed Somebody when Nobody did what Anybody could have done.

I hope reading this book has inspired, challenged, validated, and encouraged you to go beyond any preconceived definition of a school counselor and transform it into a picture of you. Whatever you do, do it with passion. It was the foundation of my entire career; it's also what grounded and energized me through good times *and* difficult times. Never give up on *any* student, no matter how frustrating or hopeless it may seem. Understand that to be an effective counselor, you have to believe that people can change their behavior. In reality, change may be inevitable, but growth is optional. As a counselor, your job is to guide your students towards the path of growth *always*. You do that by becoming a seed planter: nurturing, caring for and about, guiding, listening to, supporting, teaching, and modeling for each student. However, be content with the fact you may never know when or if the seeds sprout; still, you <u>can</u> be assured and at peace that you did "the best you knew how to do" *each* time. In doing so, you will have made and will continue to make a difference in the lives of the students you touch. In doing your best for *every* student, you will receive intangible gifts that will stay with you forever. The amazing song, "For Good," from the musical Wicked says it best: "Because I knew you, I have been changed for good." I wish you well.

Reader's Self-Analysis

Now that you've come to the end of the book, close it and return to gaze at the painting on the cover once again. Here are a series of questions to ask yourself.

Much like Where's Waldo, where are you within the boundaries of the painting?

Where did you start the journey when you began the book?

What do you deem the most important thing you've learned during this process?

What is something you want to implement, and how are you going to do it?

Finally, where do you want to go now, and how are you going to get there?

All of these answers are within YOU! May you find

fulfillment as you discover them; always remember to

    Live,

    Laugh,

    and

    Love throughout your journey.

My Warmest Regards,

Nancy

Printed in the USA
CPSIA information can be obtained
at www.ICGtesting.com
CBHW020050300424
7777CB00008B/364

9 781977 235961